GEOFF JOHNS WRITER

ETHAN VAN SCIVER PENCILLER

PRENTIS ROLLINS/MARLO ALQUIZA

MICK GRAY/ETHAN VAN SCIVER INKERS

ROB LEIGH LETTERER

MOOSE BAUMANN COLORIST

ETHAN VAN SCIVER ORIGINAL SERIES COVERS

DC COMICS

Dan DiDio VP-Executive Editor
Peter Tomasi Senior Editor-original series
Stephen Wacker Associate Editor-original series
Robert Greenberger Senior Editor-collected edition
Robbin Brosterman Senior Art Director
Paul Levitz President & Publisher
Georg Brewer VP-Design & DC Direct Creative
Richard Bruning Senior VP-Creative Director
Patrick Caldon Senior VP-Finance & Operations
Chris Caramalis VP-Finance
Terri Cunningham VP-Managing Editor
Stephanie Fierman Senior VP-Sales & Marketing
Alison Gill VP-Manufacturing
Rich Johnson VP-Book Trade Sales
Hank Kanalz VP-General Manager, WildStorm
Lillian Laserson Senior VP & General Counsel
Jim Lee Editorial Director-WildStorm
Paula Lowitt Senior VP-Business & Legal Affairs
David McKillips VP-Advertising & Custom Publishing
John Nee VP-Business Development
Gregory Noveck Senior VP-Creative Affairs
Cheryl Rubin Senior VP-Brand Management
Jeff Trojan VP-Business Development, DC Direct
Bob Wayne VP-Sales

GREEN LANTERN: REBIRTH

Published by DC Comics.

DC Comics
1700 Broadway
New York, NY 10019
A Warner Bros. Entertainment Company
Printed in Canada. First Printing.

Hardcover ISBN: 1-4012-0710-3
Softcover ISBN: 1-4012-0465-1

Cover Illustration by Ethan Van Sciver. Cover color by Moose Baumann. Logo designed by Daniel Gelon.

INTRODUCTION**BRAD MELTZER**

There were infinite ways to bring Hal Jordan back. There were simple ways ("Just give him the ring and move on already"), complex ways ("And then, if you look at *Green Lantern*, volume 2, #188 on the last page, you can see from the trees that Mogo's a healer, which'll be vital for understanding that…"), and the tried and true only-in-comics ways ("I was brainwashed." "Replaced…" "My clone…"). We, however, got the best way of all. The Geoff Johns way.

Now let me be clear here. People think *Rebirth* is about the return of Hal Jordan. And it is. But it's also about the return of Green Lantern. The Corps. The mythos. The idea that the most powerful weapon in the universe is a tiny green ring, and that each ring-bearer wields it differently. And similarly. That the ring can empower, corrupt, create, and destroy. And that the history of the spacefaring Knights of the Round Table is as vital as the present.

In lesser hands, *Rebirth* would've given us exactly what we wanted: Hal Jordan back in the costume. In Geoff's able hands, we got the return of the lore that made Hal Jordan great. You can see it on every page. From the irony of Kyle's first words in the series being, "Don't be afraid," to Sinestro's warning, "Never challenge those more powerful than you," to Hal's pitch-perfect response of, "Um…yeah. That's not gonna work for me."

With another writer, the return of Hal could've meant the death of Kyle. And, make no mistake, it would've been so easy to kill Kyle. With Geoff, we got a handshake — and introduction. Instead of plowing over the new with the past, Geoff combined the two and gave these characters something far greater: a future.

And in the center ring of this nostalgia-filled circus, littered with once-mass-murdering heroes merged with spirits of vengeance, or retribution, or whatever they called it that week, Geoff even made it all make sense. Dammit, he even took the time to explain the origin of the bomber jacket and the disappearance of Hal's once-gray hair.

But beyond all the walks down memory lane, what rang most true about *Rebirth* was the brand new nuggets that were added to the gold mine of continuity:

■ That to make the ring work, it hurts. Every time.
■ That Sinestro has to be close for the ring to translate.
■ That John's constructs are built like blueprints, that Guy's ring sprays wild, that Kyle sketches like a never-satisfied artist, that Hal just wants the precision of a good old boxing glove.
■ And my personal favorite: that Batman dislikes Hal because Hal has no fear — the one thing Batman relies on for his own "power."

In that single moment, early in issue one, I realized what a fanboy tale this is. Written by a fan. Written for the fans. For us. I love it for that. Like the character it returns, *Rebirth* has no fear embracing its own myths. Instead of trying to be cool or meta or the oh-so-popular self-aware, *Rebirth* succeeds simply because it's what all comics need to be and so often forget to be: a great story with great art.

Which, of course, brings me to the art. Why is the sci-fi craziness within these pages so believable? Because the hyper-detailed beauty of Ethan Van Sciver's art sells us every single moment. From Guy's statue in Warrior's being bigger than the rest, to the true scariness of Hector Hammond, to the fish-inspired look on Kilowog, Ethan brought it all back. This world is real. The Green Lanterns exist, and — with nothing more than sweat beading on their foreheads and skiing down their masks — they will save us. Even the chapter titles tell us so. Unlike nearly every other comic out there, Geoff and Ethan began with blackest night — and left us in brightest day. And that, as you'll see inside, is what heroes are made of.

So buckle up and start memorizing the oath. Hal Jordan hasn't just returned. He's returned to greatness.

BRAD MELTZER Ft. Lauderdale, Florida June 2005

The legacy of the Green Lantern can be traced back almost to the dawn of time. To atone for a great sin, a race of beings who came to call themselves the Guardians of the Universe sought to use great power to tame the spread of evil. After different methods failed, they settled on equipping sentient beings with rings that drew tremendous energy from a central Power Battery located on their adopted world of Oa.

The Green Lantern Corps helped to maintain peace throughout the known universe for eons. Recent events, though, saw all the Guardians but one leave this plane of existence. Soon after, the Central Battery was destroyed and the Corps shattered, all because of one man...

HAL JORDAN

Perhaps the greatest Green Lantern of them all. Test pilot Hal Jordan was bequeathed the ring and served Earth and the Corps well, but not without incident. A series of disastrous events drove Jordan past the point of mental endurance and into a crazed rampage that eventually destroyed the Corps, the Battery, and the Guardians themselves. Jordan regained his sense of purpose in time to sacrifice himself to save the Earth's dying sun. His soul has been merged with God's Spirit of Vengeance, the Spectre, and he has sought redemption before earning his final rest.

GUY GARDNER

A college football star, unable to settle on a career, Guy Gardner was selected by the Guardians to be Hal Jordan's backup. Eventually, during a cosmic crisis, Gardner earned his own ring but suffered brain damage on a mission. He healed, only to lose his ring, but discovered his DNA had been spliced with that of the alien Vuldarians. He became a living weapon and fought as Warrior until settling down, becoming proprietor and host at New York City's premier watering hole, Warriors.

JOHN STEWART

The second man chosen by Hal Jordan to act as his substitute, John Stewart didn't necessarily want to be a hero. As an architect he had a good career going, and he saw the role of Green Lantern as a distraction. In time he knew the tremendous satisfaction that came with using the ring responsibly, but after his actions led to the destruction of the planet Xanshi his spirit was crushed, and he suffered a series of ordeals that left him physically crippled as well. Recently John regained the use of his limbs, and he is now coming to terms with the traumatic incidents of his past.

KYLE RAYNER

Kyle's eagerness and fertile imagination helped him to master the power ring and adapt to his new role as Green Lantern. Eager to live up to Hal Jordan's heroic reputation, he ably handled his duties. When he attained ultimate power, Kyle, calling himself Ion, proved his humanity by using it for good, restoring the Guardians to this plane of existence. In time, though, he grew disillusioned with his effectiveness on Earth and sought to explore space. When Kyle recently returned to Earth, he saw that life had passed him by and now searches for a purpose.

ALAN SCOTT

Years ago, train engineer Alan Scott encountered an old lantern, and his life was never the same. The lantern was forged from a meteor known as the Starheart, a concentrated physical form of magical energy created in a failed attempt by the Guardians of the Universe to rid the universe of magic. Scott forged a ring from a portion of the lantern and became Earth's first Green Lantern, one of the first generation of super-heroes. He fought during World War II, switching from engineering to working at Gotham Broadcasting. Recently Scott internalized the Starheart and is now a living Lantern, imparting his wisdom to younger heroes and fighting the good fight as a member of the legendary Justice Society of America.

GANTHET

Last surviving immortal hailing back billions of years. Originally born on Maltus, he was among those who migrated to Oa and subsequently evolved into the powerful Guardians of the Universe. When the Guardians left this plane of existence, Ganthet was left behind, the final guardian of the remaining emerald energy that powered the few power rings still intact. Hal Jordan's old friend Tom Kalmaku honored his fallen comrade's last request and brought new life to Oa. Later, after being imbued with unimaginable power, Kyle Rayner expended it all to reignite the Central Power Battery. He also brought fresh life to the barren world, a new generation of Guardians. Ganthet is now raising them, teaching them of their powers and their responsibility to the universe.

NEW YORK CITY.

YOU SURE YOU DON'T WANT A DRINK? IT'S ON THE *HOUSE.*

THANKS ANYWAY.

AT LEAST THE YANKS BEAT THE BOSOX. HELLUVA GAME.

WITHOUT HIM, IT JUST FEELS LIKE THERE'S *SOMETHING* MISSING.

LOOK, MAYBE IT ISN'T *TIME* FOR HAL TO *ENJOY* LIFE. *THINK* OF WHAT HE WENT THROUGH. WHAT HE ACTUALLY *DID* AFTER COAST CITY.

THE "ONE, TRUE" GREEN LANTERN LOST ALL HIS *MARBLES.*

LIKE THE *UNIVERSE* IS A *DARKER* PLACE.

YOU WEREN'T ACTIVE WHEN IT WENT DOWN, JOHN. YOU WEREN'T THERE TO *SEE* IT.

HAL CALLED HIMSELF *PARALLAX,* HE WENT ON TRYIN' TO *REWRITE* HISTORY. KICKIN' OUR *ASSES* WHEN WE GOT IN HIS WAY.

AND THEN IT WASN'T A QUESTION OF *HAS* HAL LOST IT--

-- IT WAS A QUESTION OF DID HE *EVER* EVEN HAVE IT?

HE *HAD* IT.

THE **SPECTRE** IS AT FERRIS AIRCRAFT.

TWENTY-FIVE MILES OUTSIDE OF COAST CITY.

YOU'RE CERTAIN, ZATANNA?

HAL JORDAN'S **SOUL** HAS BEEN GRAFTED ON TO ONE OF THE MOST **POWERFUL** MYSTICAL FORCES IN EXISTENCE.

IT'S HARD **NOT** TO FEEL HIS PRESENCE WHEN HE'S WALKING THE **EARTH**. EVEN **BLUE DEVIL** COULD FIND HIM RIGHT NOW.

KEEP YOUR EYES ON GUY GARDNER, J'ONN. WE'RE GOING TO **TALK** TO HAL.

AND I'M HOPING THAT WILL BE ENOUGH.

HOPING IS WHAT YOU DO BEST, CLARK.

AND BEFORE YOU **TEAR** INTO ME AGAIN, STEWART, THAT WAS MEANT AS A COMPLIMENT.

IT MIGHT BE BETTER IF YOU STAY WITH MANHUNTER AND DOCTOR MID-NITE, QUEEN.

I'M **NOT** A **NURSE**.

AND IF THINGS GO **BAD** FOR US DOWN THERE? WHO LEADS EVERYONE **ELSE** IN?

WHO ELSE KNOWS **HAL** AS WELL AS WE DO?

I'M JUST TRYING TO **PREPARE** FOR THE **WORST**.

AND THAT'S WHAT YOU DO BEST, BATS.

...THAT'S WHAT **YOU** DO BEST.

BOOM

BOOM

BOOM

THERE WERE TWO HIKERS...THAT HELPED ME.

I HAVE RETURNED THE EARTHMEN TO THEIR DWELLINGS.

THEY ARE IN NO DANGER.

HAL JORDAN'S BODY SEEMS TO BE UNHARMED. THE RESIDUAL ENERGY HE HELD AS PARALLAX PRESERVED IT AS I BELIEVED IT MIGHT.

IN THE CENTER OF THE *SUN*...

THE SHIP YOU GAVE ME... BARELY HELD *TOGETHER.*

THE PROPER PREPARATIONS HAVE TAKEN PLACE ON OA.

I NEED TO GET TO THE LEAGUE. I NEED TO TELL THEM WHAT HAPPENED TO HAL--

THE RING--

I CAN'T... I...

IT CANNOT SNEAK UP ON *ONE* WHO *KNOWS* IT. YOUR *FLAW* HAS SPARED YOU THE FATE OF THE OTHERS.

FEAR.

BUT KILOWOG, JOHN AND GUY. IT'S ALREADY *GOTTEN* THEM.

UNDERSTOOD.

PROTECT HAL JORDAN'S BODY. HIS SOUL...

...WE MAY *YET* SAVE IT. AND THE *UNIVERSE* ITSELF.

YOU BETTER HOPE--

HOPE IS MEANINGLESS AGAINST FEAR, GREEN LANTERN OF SECTOR 2814.

FWASSHH

WILLPOWER IS OUR ONLY WEAPON.

ARRHH!

ON THE TENTH PLANET FROM THE SUN PAGALUS.

THE BEINGS THAT LIVED THERE, THEY WERE GRIPPED WITH FEAR WHEN THEY SAW MY *RING*.

ONE OF THEIR *OLDEST*, HE WAS TELLING EVERYONE THE *UNIVERSE* WAS ABOUT TO *END*...

...AT THE *HANDS* OF *PARALLAX*.

I THOUGHT HE WAS TALKING ABOUT THE *FIRST* TIME WE FOUGHT HAL TOGETHER, BUT... THEY TOLD ME THIS TALE.

A STORY ABOUT A CREATURE THAT WAS *BORN* AT THE BEGINNING OF *SENTIENCE*.

A *YELLOW* ENTITY THAT WAS MADE OF *LIVING FEAR*.

IT CREATED *TERROR* INTO ANYTHING IT CAME IN CONTACT WITH. CAUSED ENTIRE *CIVILIZATIONS* TO DESTROY THEMSELVES OUT OF *PARANOIA*.

THEIR FEAR WAS *EATEN* BY THIS CREATURE.

AND THAT CREATURE WAS CALLED *PARALLAX*.

WHAT? WHAT THE HELL ARE YOU--?

PLEASE, OLIVER. I'VE TRAVELED *LIGHT-YEARS* TO GET BACK HERE.

LET ME FINISH.

PARALLAX THREATENED TO CONSUME THE ENTIRE UNIVERSE. IT WANTED TO *INFECT* EVERY LIVING CREATURE WITH *FEAR*, AND FEAR LEADS TO *VIOLENCE*. VIOLENCE LEADS TO FEAR.

LIKE AN ENDLESS LOOP OF DEATH AND DESTRUCTION THAT WOULD KEEP *FEEDING* PARALLAX.

THEY SAID THE *GUARDIANS* KNEW PARALLAX HAD TO BE STOPPED.

WHEN THEY *FORGED* THE CENTRAL POWER BATTERY ON OA, THEY GATHERED *WILLPOWER* AS PARALLAX GATHERED *FEAR*.

THE OPPOSITE ENERGIES COULDN'T DESTROY ONE ANOTHER--

--BUT PARALLAX WAS *IMPRISONED*. PUT INTO A COMATOSE STATE THE GUARDIANS BELIEVED IT COULDN'T AWAKE FROM.

OVER THE MILLENNIA, PARALLAX BECAME KNOWN SIMPLY AS THE *YELLOW IMPURITY*. HIS *LEGEND* WAS PURPOSELY *FORGOTTEN* SO NO ONE WOULD EVER TRY TO *FREE* IT.

THAT'S WHY THE RINGS HAD A PROBLEM WITH THE COLOR *YELLOW*. PARALLAX WEAKENED ITS POWER OVER THE CORRESPONDING *SPECTRUM*.

AND ONLY SOMEONE CAPABLE OF OVERCOMING GREAT *FEAR* COULD *MASTER* THE *POWER RING*.

FOR *BILLIONS* OF YEARS, PARALLAX WAS BASICALLY *DEAD*.

AND THE *GREEN LANTERN CORPS* THRIVED.

JORDAN TRIED TO *RECREATE* COAST CITY AND WAS *REPRIMANDED* BY THE GUARDIANS. HE WAS *THREATENED,* TOLD HE MAY BE STRIPPED OF HIS POWER BECAUSE HE USED IT FOR *PERSONAL GAIN.*

SO HE DID WHAT *ANYONE* DESPERATE AND TERRIFIED WOULD DO--

--HE FOUGHT *BACK.*

AND THE TRUTH IS, I DON'T ENTIRELY BLAME HIM.

PARALLAX INFLUENCED HIM, LURING HIM BACK TO *OA.* ALONG THE WAY, JORDAN FACED OFF AGAINST HIS FELLOW CORPS MEMBERS.

ND ON OA...

...THE *GUARDIANS* PULLED A DESPERATE MOVE OF THEIR OWN. THEY FREED THE ONLY OTHER *RENEGADE, SINESTRO,* FROM THE *POWER BATTERY.* HE'D BEEN *IMPRISONED* THERE *MONTHS* EARLIER.

I'M NOT SURE WHAT THE HELL THE GUARDIANS WERE THINKING. THAT THEY'D USE THIS LUNATIC TO STOP HAL AND *THEN* PUT HIM BACK IN THE BATTERY--

--OR THAT *ONE* CORPS MEMBER WHO WENT RENEGADE COULD STOP ANOTHER?

WHATEVER THEY THOUGHT...

...THEY WERE *WRONG.*

JORDAN *BROKE* SINESTRO'S NECK.

THEN HE DESTROYED THE CENTRAL BATTERY, TAKING ALL OF THE POWER FOR HIMSELF...

AND WITHOUT EVEN KNOWING IT, JORDAN FREED *PARALLAX.*

THE COSMIC PARASITE *GRAFTED* ITSELF ON TO JORDAN'S SOUL.

AND THE PARALLAX *WE* KNOW WAS *BORN.*

IT'S BEEN THERE EVER SINCE. CORRUPTING HOW HE *THINKS.* HOW HE *ACTS.*

EVEN WHEN JORDAN RELIT THE *SUN,* AND SACRIFICED HIS LIFE TO SAVE *EARTH*--

--IT WAS JUST A MOMENTARY *GLIMPSE* OF THE REAL MAN *SHINING* THROUGH.

JOHN AND I ALWAYS WONDERED WHY MY RING NEVER HAD A PROBLEM WITH *YELLOW.*

I NEVER DREAMED IT WAS ANYTHING...NEVER THOUGHT IT *MATTERED.*

BUT IT *WORKED* BECAUSE PARALLAX WAS *FREE.*

THE YELLOW IMPURITY IS STILL *LINKED* TO HIS *SOUL?* IT'S A PART OF THE *SPECTRE* NOW?

YEAH. *EVIL* FINALLY ESCAPED JORDAN'S *SIGHT.*

IT HID *INSIDE* HIM.

THE WATCHTOWER.

HEADQUARTERS OF THE JUSTICE LEAGUE OF AMERICA.

IT ALL MAKES SENSE.

NO MATTER HOW *BAD* I DON'T WANT IT TO.

SINESTRO.

BEFORE HAL JORDAN, HE WAS CALLED THE *GREATEST* OF THE GREEN LANTERNS.

UNTIL HE PROPPED HIMSELF UP AS THE ULTIMATE *AUTHORITY* OF HIS SECTOR. HE WAS *STRIPPED* OF HIS RING AND *DISCHARGED* FROM THE CORPS.

JORDAN HELPED THE GUARDIANS DO IT.

SO SINESTRO FOUND A *DIFFERENT* RING AND A *NEW* PURPOSE.

ANNIHILATE THE *GREEN LANTERNS.*

GUY TALKS TRASH ABOUT EVERY ONE OF JORDAN'S OLD ENEMIES. ALWAYS SAYING HOW "CANDY ASS" *SONAR* IS. COUNTING THE NUMBER OF TIMES HE'S MADE *DOCTOR POLARIS* CRY. AND IT'S A *LOT.*

BUT *SINESTRO?*

GUY *NEVER* MENTIONS SINESTRO.

...KYLE RAYNER...

KRAKKKK

HIS VOICE IS *ALIEN.* *COLD* AND *HOLLOW.* AND HIS *EYES...*

IT'S LIKE TRYING TO STARE INTO THE *SUN.*

SHRAKKK

YOU *SHOULD* HAVE LET IT *BURN OUT.*

I SPEAK OF *THEM.*

DAMN.

GET READY FOR ANOTHER *SPIN.*

THE OATH ABANDONED *ME.* YOU *ALL* DID.

I *PREP* THE RING.

WHEN YOU RIPPED KORUGAR FROM MY *HANDS* YOU LEFT IT IN *CHAOS.* UNDER THE *CARE* OF A NAIVE *CHILD.*

KATMA TUI COULD NOT *REPLACE* ME.

NO ONE CAN *REPLACE* ME.

KORUGAR'S *TRUE* PROTECTOR WILL HAVE HIS *JUSTICE.*

HIS RING CRACKS.

REALITY BENDS.

I PUSH HARDER.

VWRAKOOM

IT FINALLY SHATTERS.

Heh...

JORDAN...

...WELCOME BACK.

TANGIBLE GLORY.

DO YOU EXPECT ME TO *BELIEVE* THIS?

THAT YOU WERE *INFLUENCED?* *POSSESSED?*

IS *THAT* WHAT *PARALLAX* WAS? AN OUTSIDE *FORCE* THAT--

I DON'T EXPECT *YOU* TO BELIEVE *ANYTHING.*

AND QUITE HONESTLY, I DON'T *CARE.*

When the first issue rapidly sold out, a second printing sported this variant cover.

The second issue officially sold out two weeks before hitting the shelves, so a second printing followed, using this variant cover.

I'm going to outline the basics behind what happened to Hal Jordan before getting into the miniseries outline. It's all tied into Green Lantern mythology, which is what we're looking to restore. Everything needs to be tied back into Hal Jordan, who he was, is and where he's going.

What is Parallax?

Parallax is not Hal Jordan, and never was. Parallax is the yellow impurity in the Central Power Battery. When Sinestro was imprisoned inside the Battery, he made contact with it — able to since his ring was based on the same yellow energy. On the concentrated power of fear. Sinestro gave back the yellow impurity its sentience. (The Guardians removed it when they placed it inside the Battery millions of years ago.) Sinestro manipulated Parallax, and used Parallax to corrupt Jordan and lure him to the Battery.

Hal Jordan was a target of the weapon after Coast City was destroyed — his psyche was in a vulnerable state. For the first time, he was afraid. Afraid he might not be able to stop the next catastrophe.

It was at this moment Hal was influenced by Parallax through the ring. Parallax led Hal Jordan back to Oa, and when Jordan ultimately destroyed the Corps and the Central Battery — he freed both Sinestro and Parallax. Parallax grafted completely onto its new host — Hal Jordan.

Parallax destroyed the Green Lantern Corps.

Kyle Rayner knows this, and Sinestro wants to stop him from telling the truth.

Isn't Sinestro dead?

Parallax seemingly killed Sinestro in GL #50 — but in reality, though Hal broke Sinestro's neck and left him for dead, Sinestro survived thanks to his ring. And Sinestro knew that Hal killing him would be the ultimate event in Hal's life to lead him to become wholly corrupted by Parallax. Sinestro set up his own death alongside Parallax.

Sinestro is going to be built up into a major DCU villain. Sinestro is an intergalactic anarchist, bent on toppling any kind of authority. In his eyes, no one has the right to tell others how to live — save him. And the Green Lantern Corps represent that oppression.

Sinestro doesn't want more power, he hasn't come back to destroy the world; the Spectre/Parallax is about to do that for him. He simply wants to watch his archnemesis continue to spiral down into the depths of madness.

Where is Hal Jordan's body?

When Parallax/Hal Jordan relit the sun, Hal Jordan's infected soul was separated from his body — which still lies in the center of the sun. The power of the Battery has preserved Jordan's body.

Kyle Rayner is the only person who has discovered the truth behind Parallax — in deep space he came across one of the oldest surviving races of sentient beings in the galaxy. Their original home planet had been destroyed by what they called the source of fear. An entity called Parallax that was created by fear. That feeds off fear, and continues to grow. Parallax is a legend in the far corner of the universe.

Kyle retrieved Hal's body from the sun and headed to Earth.

Kyle will be a major key in clearing Hal's name — and when Hal returns as Green Lantern in issue #5, it is with Kyle that he'll team up.

Why did the Spectre choose Hal Jordan as a host?

The Spectre force specifically grafted itself onto the soul of Hal Jordan, and laid the seeds in the minds of the others to find Hal's soul — because the Spectre hoped to "burn out" this monster of fear. The Spectre believed that his power combined with Hal's willpower could destroy Parallax.

(This is where our story opens. Not only has the Spectre failed to annihilate Parallax, but the Parallax force is beginning to corrupt the Spectre's power.)

Who is Hal Jordan?

Hal Jordan is not afraid to fail. Hal believes he can handle anything that's thrown at him. He'll venture into any threatening situation without hesitation.

The Parallax weapon has planted doubts in Hal's mind. Doubts he must shred to overcome it.

Hal's greatest asset has always been his willpower, his belief that he can accomplish anything, and he's going to get that back.

How will Hal Jordan return to the land of the living?

The Spectre can no longer contain Hal's poisoned soul. The Parallax force is overwhelming him and causing chaos across the Earth. In a way, the Spectre must perform a massive cosmic self-"abortion" of sorts that will be witnessed by crowds of our heroes.

As Hal/Parallax is literally torn from within Spectre's body, ripped by Spectre's own claws and covered in a greenish blood, Hal and Parallax separate — then Parallax leaps back inside Spectre. Hal's soul fades from sight as it is called to the afterlife.

Fading away, Hal watches helplessly as Parallax burrows like a parasite back into Spectre. Hal's soul disappears, spinning towards the "light at the end of the tunnel."

But Spectre sends a blast towards Hal's soul, redirecting it — sending it back into his body. The white light in the tunnel turns green.

Hal Jordan will awake in his body, which was brought back to Earth by Kyle.

How will Hal Jordan be absolved in the eyes of our heroes?

If Hal Jordan killed one person, there *may* be a chance at redemption. As Parallax he killed dozens more. We need to absolve him of this. He can have the potential inside him, which was exploited, but he cannot be responsible for these actions.

When the Parallax force is torn from the Spectre, it infects another hero — Batman. Since Hal went "bad," Batman has been the loudest voice denouncing him. We want to bring this to a close for several reasons, the main one being – it's time to move on.

If Batman stays suspicious of Hal Jordan, we'll have to remind the readers about the Spectre, Parallax, etc. We want to start as clean as possible. To us, this was just one story in Hal's life. We're moving on to the next.

Ultimately, it will be Kyle Rayner who is the voice that convinces everyone Hal is back.

NOTE: Parallax only corrupts power, it has none of its own. So inside Batman, it simply corrupts Batman and his inherent abilities.

We want to keep all of this as simple and connected as possible, we want to reach a strong status quo of Hal Jordan as a Green Lantern after this series. His journey will not be one of redemption or guilt, but one of rebuilding.

Rebuilding Hal's life, rebuilding Coast City, rebuilding the Corps, rebuilding a hero. Our theme for the monthly book.

THE ISSUE BREAKDOWNS — I'll be going into much more detail on issue #1. Obviously, scenes will evolve and change slightly during scripting.

ISSUE ONE (30 PAGES)

Pages 1 through 5

We open in space. Space Sector 2814. High above Earth. Suddenly, a space-craft, brittle and burning, flies past us. As if it were bursting out of the sun...

Heading towards Earth.

The craft smashes through the atmosphere, breaking apart. It crashes in the Southwestern desert, skidding across the ground. A pair of hikers see it and approach the craft.

They walk into the hull through a hole and find the pilot.

The pilot is Kyle Rayner. Like Abin Sur years earlier when he has crashed on Earth.

Kyle's costume is phasing in and out. He quickly awakens, claws at his costume, wants it off. Kyle passes out.

A large metal chest-like object is next to him.

Pages 6 through 9

Cut to John Stewart and Hal Jordan. They are approaching Yankee Stadium, surrounded by people. John urges Hal to enjoy himself, finally glad he's agreed to appear in public. To try and become human again. Hal looks on, can hear the people's sins and remorse all around him. It's hard to tune it out, the Spectre's job is never done. He's not supposed to rest. Technically...he's dead.

John convinces Hal to stay and watch the game. Hal actually begins to enjoy himself. Then Hal can't help but ask how Carol is doing.

She's with her new husband. She's fine.

Suddenly, all around them, people are confessing their sins. A husband tells his wife he cheated on her. A man on his cell-phone calls his boss and admits embezzling money. Even John admits that he helped his ex-girlfriend get a job with the D.E.O. because in a way it was easier to break up. John is slightly dizzy. Hal realizes the Spectre will not let him rest...no time for himself. The Spirit of Vengeance calls out.

Hal changes into the Spectre and disappears, leaving a very confused crowd. John is concerned.

Page 10

Cut to Carol Ferris at Ferris Aircraft, brought in to rebuild the company. She's on the phone with her husband, Gil. He's in Chicago on business. Carol feels something is watching her — turns, but the shadow is gone. A passenger plane takes off for the Coast.

Pages 11 through 15

Star City. Green Arrow is investigating a strange occurrence in the city with Arsenal and Connor Hawke. Before they can even begin to wonder where the three men are — they get a call from Speedy. Someone's broken into *their* house.

They race to Oliver's home where Mia is fighting with Black Hand — a Green Lantern villain who was always after his ring. He's tracked the extra power ring given to Green Arrow by Hal Jordan.

Suddenly, Spectre shows up — helps Green Arrow take down Black Hand.

Hal reverts to normal — he wants to have a talk with Green Arrow. "No once could challenge me like you could, Ollie." Hal is very cold toward Arsenal and Connor — telling them to leave. They argue, but Hal waves his hand — sending them away.

Hal feels he's losing himself to the Spirit of Vengeance. He feels he's very close — but when Black Hand attacks Green Arrow, Oliver sees a very different Hal Jordan. He transforms into the Spectre and destroys Black Hand in a hideous way. Spectre disappears.

Green Arrow picks up the power ring Black Hand was after, concerned.

Pages 16 through 18

Cut to Warrior's Bar in New York. It's 3 a.m. Guy Gardner is cleaning the bar, kicks the last drunk out, reminiscing about his life as a Green Lantern with John Stewart. Guy looks over the display — we get a sense of history here. And a sense of how much Hal meant to Guy in reality. "He was never afraid. Could even pick out the most beautiful girl in a bar and walk right up to her."

Guy suddenly begins to feel sick. The yellow power ring on his finger (established in SUPER FRIENDS) crackles with energy.

There's a huge explosion as he takes out the entire bottom section of the building. Warriors' Bar is gone. John rises from the ashes with a badly hurt Guy Gardner. The yellow ring crackled.

Pages 19 through 20

Cut to the Ferris Passenger Aircraft. The pilot flies over what was once Coast City, we get some history here. What happened to the City, how it was destroyed. Suddenly, a flash of green light goes off. And then they see something odd.

Down below, all the roadways, signs, etc. are in place. Only one building stands. A large sign reads: Welcome to Coast City.

The people can't believe this.

Page 21

Cut to Belle Reve, where Hector Hammond, criminal psychic, is acting strangely. Normally, he is unable to move. But he's muttering.

"I know the truth now. I know the truth"

"There are three voices, not two."

Pages 22 through 28

At the JLA Watchtower — Batman, the Atom, John Stewart and others — all examining Guy Gardner's damaged body. Trying to analyze him and find out what is wrong. The yellow ring won't come off.

INTERCUT WITH

Batman is in communication with another group of heroes — Aquaman and others — who are investigating the mysterious building in Coast City. No one can explain what is going on. There is only one building standing. (Aquaman also mentions how the sea life in the waters along Coast City has all but disappeared.)

Batman becomes very concerned after he gets the "address" of the one building in Coast City — it's Hal Jordan's old apartment building, where he lived after being kicked out of the Air Force. And Guy Gardner is wounded. Batman asks, "Where's Hal Jordan?"

A talk between Batman and John — John defending Hal. Arguments of the heroes back and forth about Hal Jordan.

Another group of heroes, including Superman and Alan Scott, in New York, clearing out what was once Warrior's Bar. Mysteries deepen as they find one object has survived the blast.

Standing all alone — a statue of HAL JORDAN, GREEN LANTERN. Untouched and protected.

Alan Scott feels slightly ill as he gets close to the statue. Has to retreat.

Back on the Watchtower, Green Arrow beams aboard. Tells them about his encounter with Hal Jordan. The third strike for Batman. He gets on the JLA communicator, warns everyone.

"Everyone go to red alert. The *real* Hal Jordan is back."

Pages 29 and 30

Cut to Ferris Aircraft. Southern California.

Carol steps out of her office — on the runway, among the planes is

HAL JORDAN.

It begins to rain.

ISSUE TWO
THE BASICS: Hal Jordan has seemingly gone to the dark side again, and the heroes of the world reluctantly unite against him. Meanwhile, Green Lanterns (including John, Guy and Alan) are corrupted and begin turning against their fellow heroes as Kyle Rayner is hunted by a former friend, Kilowog.

We open on something flying through space — glowing green. Heading towards Earth. We don't know who yet. (This is Kilowog, influenced by Parallax using the Spectre's power, hunting down Kyle Rayner.)

Cut to Kyle Rayner. At a camp site. Being taken care of by the hikers. They're looking at the metal chest. Trying to get it to open. They have no idea who the hell this guy is, the spaceship, any of it. A pickup truck is nearby, the chest/coffin loaded in back. On the chest they find a strange pseudo-futuristic tablet. A PARALLAX symbol on it.

Cut to Carol and Hal at Ferris Aircraft — Hal looking to Carol for help. Hal admits his guilt and erratic thoughts and actions of late – especially his self-doubt and fear. Recounts what he used to be like before Coast City, and how he can't understand where his feelings went. Or where the fear came from.

Carol's cell phone rings — Batman. He tells Carol to keep calm, keep Hal there.

The JLA and some reserves appear before Hal. All signs point to Hal going mad with power again. A massive battle between the Spectre and the heroes. John Stewart is corrupted with Alan Scott as they side with the Spectre against the heroes. Hal is barely able to control himself. *Fear* taking him over.

INTERCUT WITH: Inside the JLA HQ, Guy Gardner returns as a Green Lantern (a ring created by John's is put on his finger to destroy the yellow ring), resulting in a fight in the Watchtower. Guy heads towards Earth, joining up with the rest of the "evil" Green Lantern Corps — John and Alan.

Cut to the Southwest. Kyle Rayner awakens with the hikers. He struggles to use his ring, keeping the power level low — he could be detected or, if he uses too much, taken over. He's acting mad. Suddenly, the hikers are incinerated by a green beam from above. Kilowog, influenced by the Parallax force (though we don't know this yet), flies in for the kill, calling Kyle a traitor.

A fight begins, Kyle barely holding his own — struggling not to use the ring. He can feel it infect him. During the fight, the chest/coffin is blown open. And inside —

The body of Hal Jordan, Parallax.

ISSUE THREE
THE BASICS: Kyle goes to his father's home for help while Hal is confronted by the Spectre force, believing the Spectre is corrupting him. Meanwhile, the true nature of Parallax is revealed as Sinestro makes his presence known. Essentially — the "everyone learns the TRUE origin of Parallax" issue.

We open in the home of Kyle Rayner's father. Kyle reaches his father, bloody and beaten, looking for help. He needs to get to the nearest JLA teleportation tube. He's barely escaped Kilowog.

Heroes across the world are suiting up to battle it out with the Spectre and the Green Lantern Corps. The corrupted Corps members have each begun to act out their own fearful fantasies as Hal Jordan did. Guy takes on his former League members, focusing on Batman, John destroying every structure he ever designed (his being an architect will play a large role in GL later on, in the rebuilding of Coast City), etc. Reactions of everyone as they believe another "Zero Hour" or "Crisis" is coming. Some are disappointed (Arsenal), others not surprised (Nightwing).

Hector Hammond continues to freak out, causing Batman to investigate with Martian Manhunter, attempting to learn what Hammond knows about the truth.

As the Green Lanterns make their attacks on the heroes, Hal searches for the true culprit behind these acts — and upon reaching Coast City, discovers that it is himself.

Meanwhile, Kyle and his father briefly bond as Kyle reveals everything to his dad. Who he is, what he does, etc. (Per the GL comic, Kyle's dad already knows he is Green Lantern, though Kyle is unaware of this.) Kyle and his father will head to one of many "secret" teleportation spots the JLA has scattered across the country.

Kyle and his father head to the Watchtower, nothing there. It's all messed up. They find one hero still somewhat conscious, Green Arrow. Green Arrow asks what the hell is going on. Green Arrow still has the power ring, which saved his life. Kyle tells him not to use it — it'll take him over. "What will?" Kyle recounts the story of Parallax — utilizing flashbacks. We'll see Kyle's journey in deep space — the world he found — the legend of Parallax — etc. The Parallax force is fear.

Intercut with: In Coast City, where Hal is being hunted by everyone, confronts the Spectre force, learns of Parallax. "How did I become afraid?" asks Hal. **"Evil escaped your sight. It hid within you."** The Spectre force tells him Parallax is too powerful.

Back to the Watchtower. Green Arrow asks who freed this Parallax thing. Who's behind it? Suddenly, a yellow bow and arrow appears — shooting Green Arrow in the chest. Walking out of the darkness, a smile on his face. The master of the yellow ring — Sinestro.

ISSUE FOUR.
The Basics: Kyle battles Sinestro while Spectre struggles to free himself of Hal Jordan's soul.

A massive battle between Kyle and Sinestro erupts. (Think of it like the first time Darth Vader, Sinestro, battled Luke Skywalker, Kyle. Darth Vader barely moves, using one hand on his light saber while Luke sweats, struggling to hold on to his.) Kyle's father saves Green Arrow's life. Kyle not only has to protect his father and Green Arrow, he also must ward off the influence of the ring.

As Kyle fights Sinestro, he tells Green Arrow to take his father and find the JLA. Tell them the truth about Hal.

The Spectre has lost control, struggling to keep the Parallax force in check. More scenes of Spectre/Hal/Parallax acting out — threatening lives (from Hal Jordan's friends and family to his villains).

Intercut with Green Arrow. He makes contact with Batman, joins up with him at Belle Reve. Entire truth is told, though Batman is still reluctant to believe it — and even if it is true, Hal should've overpowered it. Zatanna helps locate the Spectre and the JLA. Kyle's father is worried about his son.

On the Watchtower, the fight continues. Kyle is beaten to Hell by Sinestro. Sinestro leaves the Watchtower — sensing the moment of Hal's ultimate failure is at hand.

Intercut with the Spectre "aborting" Hal Jordan and Parallax from his body. Hal's soul watching helplessly as Parallax stays, gripping Spectre. When we see the Parallax force we see that it is yellow. (Setting this up for when Parallax is thrust back into the Power Battery.)

Sinestro arrives just in time to witness this and see Hal.

Hal fades away — heading towards a bright white light. Spectre hits Hal with some kind of energy…but Hal disappears. Heading towards the bright light.

ISSUE FIVE. (30 PAGES)
The Basics: Hal reawakens in his own body, joins forces with Kyle and heads to retake the Parallax force himself, believing he knows how to destroy it.

We open with Hal traveling through the white light, suddenly the white light turns a deep green.

HAL IS REBORN

Hal wakes up in his body, still in the coffin on the Watchtower. He coughs, pukes…his hair is brown from here on out. Hal looks down at his body, pulls his armor off piece by piece. He can't stand wearing the Parallax uniform. (We learn the Spectre directed his soul to the body, knowing Hal could help him.)

Hal finds Kyle, wounded badly but still ready to fight. They need to get back to Earth.

Hal sees a statue of himself — wearing his old costume. Time for a quick change.

Meanwhile, on Earth, Hal and Kyle free the Green Lantern Corps members from Parallax's control.

Kyle and the Green Lanterns versus Spectre/Parallax versus Sinestro, DCU heroes help. Sinestro is beaten, but flees back home to Qward. Hal gets Parallax free from Spectre with the help of the rest of the Corps members.

The Spectre is cleansed but Parallax survives, infects Batman.

The Spectre force does not stay to help, like the ending of *Raiders of the Lost Ark*, the Spectre force spirals into the sky.

Many other heroes hurt, are unable to follow Parallax/Batman. Hal tells all the powerful ones to leave this to the "mortals," including him. If Parallax gets in Captain Marvel or Wonder Woman, this fight will go to an entirely different level.

Batman is hunted down by Jordan, Green Arrow, Nightwing, Robin, Black Canary, etc. Batman attacks Jim Gordon, ex-Commissioner. He takes his gun. But shooting a criminal isn't what shows Batman how impossible it is to resist Parallax.

Robin is there, trying to stop Batman. He gets in Batman's way — tells him to put the gun down. This isn't him.

Batman shoots Robin.

Right in the shoulder, Robin falls to the ground. Bleeding.

Hal — normal human form — stops Batman from firing again. A massive fight. Hal gets his ring back from Green Arrow. Parallax leaves Batman, heads back into Hal Jordan.

Everyone waits with bated breath — Hal's about to become Parallax again. But something happens this time — Parallax has no fear to take hold of. Hal's not afraid anymore — and Hal forces Parallax back out.

Together — with all of the GL's — they pronounce the Oath and break apart Parallax, each one sending him back into the rings, imprisoning Parallax back into the Central Battery.

Epilogues:
There'll be many epilogues — between Hal and the Lanterns, Hal and Green Arrow, Hal and Batman & the JLA, etc. (A major moment where Batman apologizes to Hal Jordan — he understands what he went through now. Robin is healing.)

Kyle will head into space with Kilowog and his father. He and his father have made a connection, and Kyle's father has always wanted to fly among the stars.

Hal standing in Coast City, looking up at the building. Deciding it is time to rebuild.

The last three pages will be on Oa. The Guardians on Oa gather together, age and nod in agreement. It is time to rebuild here as well.

"It is time."

THE BEGINNING.

BIOGRAPHIES

GEOFF JOHNS

Geoff Johns was born on January 25, 1973 in Detroit. It was damn cold.

He attended Michigan State University and studied media arts, screenwriting, film production and theory. After graduating, Geoff moved to Los Angeles where he made a lucky phone call and got a job as an intern for Richard Donner. He then went on to become Donner's assistant for almost four years on Conspiracy Theory and *Lethal Weapon 4*. During that time, he bean writing comics beginning with his favorite title, STARS AND S.T.R.I.P.E., which he created for DC. Eventually, writing turned into a full-time career.

Geoff has written INFINITE CRISIS, THE FLASH, TEEN TITANS, JSA, HAWKMAN, JLA/JSA: VIRTUE & VICE and various other titles for DC Comics and *The Avengers* for Marvel. He lives with his wife, Anissa, in Southern California, still writing for comics and television.

ETHAN VAN SCIVER

Ethan Van Sciver, born on September 3, 1974, has been drawing comics and comic book characters since he was 4 years old. Back then, DC wouldn't return his phone calls. Now look at him. He's working with the best writer, inker, colorist and editorial team in the business. Persistence is key.

At home, Ethan likes to watch terrible old movies, listen to surf music and play Hot Wheels with his son, Hunter. He blames his expanding waistline on the fabulous gourmet cooking of his wife Shari, but it's also probably due to a lot of long workdays putting more lines on Sinestro's face and eating cookies.

His artistic influences are Brian Bolland, Bernie Wrightson, Jack Cole, John Byrne and Todd McFarlane, and his goal in comics is to produce an amazing Plastic Man book one day. We'll see!

PRENTIS ROLLINS

Prentis Rollins has been inking comics since 1993. His credits include *Touch*, *New X-Men*, POWER COMPANY, JLA: INCARNATIONS, IMPULSE, DC ONE MILLION, BATMAN: THE ULTIMATE EVIL and HARDWARE. He is cofounder of Monkeysuit Press. Prentis lives in New York City with his wife and daughter.

MARLO ALQUIZA

Marlo was born in 1970, raised on comics, *Star Wars*, and toys. After graduating with a degree in art from U.C. Berkeley in 1993, he entered the comics industry first working for Image Comics (*Prophet, Darkchylde*, etc). He subsequently went freelance and worked with Top Cow (*Darkness, Rising Stars, Tomb Raider*), and Marvel (*X-Men*). After joining DC, Marlo's work has been found in CATWOMAN, ACTION COMICS and most recently TEEN TITANS. Married, he has a five-year-old daughter and four-year-old son.

MICK GRAY

Mick Gray has been inking comics for nearly 16 years. He has inked many DC titles including HAWKMAN, CHASE, DETECTIVE, ZATANNA, LEGION OF SUPER-HEROES, JLA ADVENTURES, AQUAMAN, SON OF SUPERMAN and PROMETHEA, for which he won an Eisner Award in 2001. He lives in San Jose, California with his wife, Holly, and daughter, Genevieve.

ROB LEIGH

Rob Leigh is a graduate of the Joe Kubert School. His lettering first received critical notice in 1972, when he was sent home with a note for writing a four-letter word on the blackboard of Miss Tuschmann's second-grade class. In addition to lettering, Rob has inked many titles for DC. He lives in northern New Jersey with his wife, Vaughan, and homicidal cat, Barley.

MOOSE BAUMAN

Having puttered around the industry for several years, Moose finally gained credibility and respect by joining DC Comics' stable of creators. He's worked on the monthly GREEN LANTERN series, ACTION COMICS, BLOODHOUND, and HUMAN DEFENSE CORPS, to name just a few. He currently lives with his family in a concrete bunker in Northern California.